AGAINST THE GODS?

A Concise Guide to Atheism and Agnosticism

STEFAN MOLYNEUX

ISBN: 1975654382
ISBN 13: 9781975654382

Contents

Foreword

Escaping the Cave: Philosophy, Agnosticism, and the Academy

Philosophy has lost its way: Graduate students and faculty research ever more obscure and inconsequential topics; students speak in vernacular that insulates their arguments from criticism because nobody can understand what they're saying; paths of philosophical inquiry are blocked by diversity boards; professors are held hostage to political correctness, etc. Worse still, philosophy as it's found in the academy has become a culture of pretending – pretending one understands arguments one does not and pretending that obfuscation is a sign of intellectual virtue.

Rather than attempting to eradicate these disturbing values, academic philosophers have institutionalized them. Where there was once free expression, genuine inquiry, and an emphasis on clarity and rigor, now there's limited expression, hampered inquiry, and an emphasis on issues that matter to almost nobody except the very, very few philosophers who study them.

It's no surprise, then, that it would take someone from outside the academy to write with clarity, purpose, and freedom of expression; someone who doesn't attempt to stupefy readers, or to protect them from offense, but to clear up complicated issues so that literally billions of people can align their beliefs with reality.

In *Against the Gods*, Molyneux isn't concerned with people's feelings, or about showing how smart he is by using terms few outside of academic philosophy understand, or about being shut down by offices of diversity, equity, and inclusion, or about not upsetting anyone so he'll have a chance at tenure, or about pretending to know things he doesn't so his peers will show their approbation.

Against the Gods is a crystal clear, honest, sincere, and blunt roadmap out of the morass of agnosticism and poor ways of thinking. It lays out arguments about God, agnosticism, the supernatural, religion as child abuse, etc., that anyone can understand and act upon to lead a better life. *Against the Gods* is a tonic. It's an analeptic read that calls upon one to be honest with oneself about one's beliefs – specifically one's beliefs about God.

Where *Against the Gods* shines most brightly is in the linguistic and conceptual analysis of agnosticism. Agnosticism, as Molyneux argues, is a position of intellectual and even emotional cowardice. He's right. Agnosticism is a cop-out. It's a position people profess to adopt because they're too fearful of the alternative (a godless universe), or too dishonest and insincere with themselves, or too afraid to offend others with the term "atheist."

Against the Gods is a nail in agnosticism's coffin. Molyneux is a pallbearer. Once we can finally and permanently put agnosticism to rest, we can turn our attention to an even more pernicious scourge – faith. Molyneux has begun this journey for us by making an extraordinarily contribution to the much-overlooked dangers of agnosticism.

Public intellectuals like Molyneux, unencumbered by rigid, culturally shifting rules and arbitrary intellectual boundaries of academic philosophy departments, are agents of real, profound change in a much larger, much more meaningful landscape. *Against the Gods* is an outsider's philosophy book, uncharacteristic in its forthright nature and bold in its lack of pretension. It will indelibly alter your understanding of gods.

Peter Boghossian
Philosophy Department
Portland State University
A Manual for Creating Atheists
@peterboghossian

Introduction

While strolling through the sunny woods one day, you spy a man slithering through the undergrowth, heavily camouflaged and gripping a bow and arrow.

"What are you hunting?" you ask.

"Dragons!" hisses the man proudly.

You frown. "Dragons? But dragons don't exist!"

The man nods emphatically. "I completely agree with you! There ain't *no such thing* as dragons. And I'm a-gonna *shoot* me one!" He raises his bow and arrow, narrows his eyes and glares through the trees, hungry to target the non-existent.

At this point, you would surely take a series of slow and steady steps back-wards, aiming to put some safer distance between you and a deranged man wielding a bow and arrow.

This is one of the many, many challenges of atheism.

"Atheism" is a terrible word on many levels.

The Oxford English Dictionary, Second Edition, defines atheism as:

"Disbelief in, or denial of, the existence of a god."

To any modern, rational thinker, this is an entirely unsatisfactory definition – which is exactly what you expect from a word originally defined by theists.

First of all, the OED definition implies that there is something *personal* in the rational rejection of a god. "Denial" is a word associated with defensive rejections of reality, such as Holocaust denier, climate change denier – or the generic avoidance of unpalatable emotional truths: "He's in denial about her drinking."

Compare the above definition to this one:

"Atheism: The acceptance of the non-existence of imaginary entities such as Santa Claus, the Easter Bunny and Bronze Age sky ghosts."

The difference should be clear.

Also, why is the phrase *"a* god" used? If I say that supernatural beings such as leprechauns do not exist, why would anyone imagine that I only disbelieved in a single leprechaun named "Bob"?

Rational thinkers have nothing against any *particular* deity – any more than a mathematician dislikes in *particular* the proposition that two and two make five. If such a mathematician existed, and loudly proclaimed his opposition to that particular equation, and founded a society called "against two and two making five," he would be considered beyond eccentric, and it would be generally understood that he had utterly failed to grasp the most basic principles of mathematics.

A thinker cannot logically differentiate the nonexistence of a *deity* from the nonexistence of any other thing which does not exist. Principles by definition apply in *general,* rather than in particular, just as a method of long division cannot only apply to one particular combination of numbers.

The criteria for existence versus nonexistence is a *general* standard, which applies equally to rocks, electricity, electrons, ghosts, dreams, square circles, concepts and unicorns. It cannot rationally focus its energies on only *one* entity – or even one category – otherwise it becomes mere prejudice, rather than the dispassionate application of a general principle.

Defining "atheism" as being "against the gods" is thus a misnomer, since it takes a merely accidental subset of a larger set of principles and turns it into an arbitrary principle itself. There is no such thing as being "against the existence of gods," any more than there is such a thing as being "anti-leprechaun." In fact, to say that you are against one leprechaun *in particular* is to imply that you *believe* in leprechauns overall, but find one of them in particular somehow offensive.

We cannot rationally be "against gods," just as we cannot be "against" square circles, or hostile to the idea of gravity in the absence of mass, or offended by the idea that human beings can live unaided on the surface of the sun. These propositions are simply false, according to reason and evidence, and to create a second category of particular offense "against the gods" is irrational – and, fittingly enough, offensive, due to the implied prejudice.

Rational thinkers accept standards of existence that at least involve logical consistency – and with any luck, empirical evidence. It is the first standard that beliefs in gods fail and – as a result, there is little point looking for the second.

The word "atheist" also indicates that belief in gods is the standard, and atheism is the exception – just as "sane" is the standard, and "insane" is the exception. This is a mere scrap of sophistic propaganda, since all theists are almost complete atheists, in that they do not believe in the vast majority of man's gods. The rejection of gods is the default position; the acceptance of a deity remains extremely rare, though not as rare as atheists would like.

THE EXISTENCE OF GODS

Two main errors are generally made when examining the existence of gods.

The first is to ignore the basic fact that gods cannot logically exist, and the second is to accept such logical impossibilities, but to create some imaginary realm where gods *may* exist. Broadly speaking, the first error is made by theists, who argue that gods do exist, and the second by agnostics, who argue that they may exist.

In the first instance, gods are viewed as similar to unicorns. If we define a unicorn as a horse with a horn on its head, we cannot logically say that such a creature can never exist. There may be such a being on some other planet, or in some undiscovered place in this world, or perhaps a mutation may arise at some point in the future which pushes a horn out of the forehead of a standard-issue horse.

The concept of a horse with a horn on its head is not logically self-contradictory – and thus such a being may exist, and it would be foolish to state otherwise.

In the same way, life forms based on silicon rather than carbon may exist somewhere in the universe – such beings are not logically self-contradictory, and so their existence cannot be rationally eliminated.

However, if I define a unicorn as a horse with a horn on its head that can fly through interstellar space, go backwards through time powered by its magical rainbow tail, and which existed prior to the universe – well, then we have moved into another category of assertion entirely.

A horse cannot live in space, since there is no oxygen, or air pressure, or water – and about a thousand other reasons. The properties and necessities of carbon-based life forms *completely eliminate* such a possibility.

A being which does not contradict the properties of existence may exist – a proposed being which does, may not.

Bertrand Russell argued for agnosticism by saying that there may be a little teapot orbiting somewhere in the solar system, but he considered it highly unlikely. This argument – with all due respect to Dr. Russell's genius – is incorrect. A teapot is *not* a self-contradictory entity. If I could communicate with Dr. Russell in his current state of nonexistence, I would ask him whether he would consider it possible that an eternal living horse was floating somewhere in deep space – and I respect his knowledge of biology enough to be sure that he would answer in the negative.

Gods are not like little teapots, or horses with horns, or very small Irishman with pots of gold – gods are entirely self-contradictory entities, the supernatural equivalent of square circles.

We do not have to hunt the entire universe to know that a square circle cannot exist, because it is a self-contradictory concept. We do not have to examine every rock on every planet to know that a rock cannot fall up and down at the same time. We do not have to count every object in the universe to know that two and two make four, not five. There is no possibility that self-contradictory entities can exist anywhere in the universe. We know that an object cannot be a teacup and an armchair and a horse with a horn at the same time. The Aristotelian laws of identity and non-contradiction deny us the luxury of believing that self-contradictory entities exist anywhere except in our own unreliable imaginations.

WHY ARE GODS
SELF-CONTRADICTORY?

At the very minimum, a god is defined as an eternal being which exists independent of material form and detectable energy, and which usually possesses the rather enviable attributes of omniscience and omnipotence.

First of all, we know from biology that even if an eternal being *could* exist, it would be the simplest being conceivable. An eternal being could never have evolved, since it does not die and reproduce, and therefore biological evolution could never have layered levels of increasing complexity over its initial simplicity. We all understand that the human eye did not pop into existence without any prior development; and the human eye is infinitely less complex than an omniscient and omnipotent god. Since gods are portrayed as the most complex beings imaginable, they may well be many things, but eternal cannot be one of them.

Secondly, we also know that consciousness is an *effect* of matter – specifically biological matter, in the form of a brain. Believing that consciousness can exist in the absence of matter is like believing that gravity can be present in the absence of mass, or that light can exist in the absence of a light source, or that electricity can exist in the absence of energy. Consciousness is an effect of matter, and thus to postulate the existence of consciousness without matter is to create an insurmountable paradox, which only proves the nonexistence of what is being proposed.

If you doubt this, try telling your friends that that no woman can bear your company – and that you have a girlfriend. Having a girlfriend is an *effect* of female company, just as consciousness is an effect of brain matter. Alternatively, try speaking to someone without making a sound or a movement. Speaking is an effect of movement, either in the vocal chords or somewhere else, and therefore it cannot exist in the absence of motion. (If someone insists that consciousness can exist without a brain, ask them to demonstrate the proposition without using his brain.)

Thirdly, omniscience cannot coexist with omnipotence, since if a god knows what will happen tomorrow, said god will be unable to change it without invalidating its knowledge. If this god retains the power to change what will happen tomorrow, then it cannot know with exact certainty what will happen tomorrow.

The usual response from theists – it is impossible to use the word 'answer' – is to place their god "outside of time," but this is pure nonsense. When an entity is proven to be self-contradictory, creating a realm wherein self-contradictions are valid *does not solve the problem*. If you tell me that a square circle cannot exist, and I then create an imaginary realm called "square circles can exist," we are not at an impasse; I have just abandoned reality, rationality and quite possibly my sanity.

Theists who try this particular con should at least be consistent, and not pay their taxes, and then, when said taxes are demanded, say to the tax collector that they have created a universe called "I paid my taxes," and slam the door in his face. (Alternatively, if theists make a mistake on a history test, and claim that the American Revolution was in 1676, they should fight the resulting bad mark by claiming that their answer exists "outside of time.")

The fourth objection to the existence of deities is that an object can only rationally be defined as existing when it can be detected in some manner, either directly, in the form of matter and/or energy, or indirectly, based upon its effects on the objects around it, such as a black hole.

That which can be detected is that which exists, as anyone who has tried walking through a glass door can painfully tell you. Such a door is deemed to be open – or nonexistent – when we can walk through it without detecting the glass with our soon-to-be-bloody nose. It would be epistemological madness to argue that an open door is synonymous with a closed door. If someone argues that existence is equal to nonexistence, challenge them to walk through a wall rather than an archway. (The fact that the wall might be an archway in another dimension will scarcely help their passage in this one.)

Differentiating between existence and nonexistence was something that my daughter was able to manage before she was 6 months old; we can only hope that modern philosophical thinkers are able to circle back and someday achieve her prodigious feats of knowledge.

A god – or at least any god that has been historically proposed or accepted – is that which cannot be detected by any material means, either directly or indirectly.

Ah, but what about the future? Might we find gods orbiting Betelgeuse in the 25th century? Well, while it is true that at some point we may come across some seemingly magical being somewhere in the universe that may appear somewhat godlike to us, no one who has proposed the existence of gods in the past has ever met such a being, which we can tell because no test for existence has ever been proposed or accepted.

Since "god" means "that which is undetectable, either directly or indirectly," then the statement "gods exist" rationally breaks down to:

"That which does not exist, exists."

Thus not only is the concept of gods entirely self-contradictory, but even the proposition that they exist is self-contradictory.

Other Dimensions

Theists claim that gods exist, atheists accept that they do not; agnostics say that gods are unlikely, but not impossible.

How do they manage this?

Many agnostics understand that gods do not – and cannot – exist in physical reality, so they create "Dimension X," and place the possibility of gods existing somewhere "out there." Inevitably, when a rational thinker points out that this does not solve the problem, the agnostic replies with grating haughtiness that the rational thinker is being closed-minded, and sniffs that to claim the nonexistence of any particular entity is short-sighted and unimaginative. "Surely," he says, "if you were to tell a medieval man that human beings would one day be able to talk instantaneously around the world, he would say that such a feat was utterly impossible – but he would be only exposing the limitations of his more primitive mind, not making any objective truth statement."

In other words, any and all certainty is primitive superstition.

This wonderful piece of sophistry is a patently ridiculous form of *ad hominem*, which goes something like this:

"Just as Newtonian physics gave way to Einsteinian physics, and Einsteinian physics was in some ways surpassed by quantum mechanics, making absolute truth statements about all forms of future knowledge shows a deep ignorance of the flexible and progressive nature of the scientific method, and the endless potential for human thought."

This is a very strange notion, in which the scientific method is used to pave the way not *away* from ghosts, demons and a generally haunted universe, but rather *towards* it. The science of medicine has attempted to escape the primitive foolishness of witch doctors and the superstitions of demonic possession – to say that true medicine leads us towards such primitive fantasies, rather than helping us escape them, entirely misunderstands the purpose of science, reason and medicine.

Of course it is true that Newtonian physics gave way to Einsteinian physics, and Einsteinian physics may well be surpassed by some other approach – to say so is boringly obvious. However, reason and evidence is a *process*, it is not any specific *content*. Science is a *method*, not a specific theory or proposition. It is only reason and evidence that *reveals* the superiority of more accurate and comprehensive theories. The scientific method rejects self-contradictory theories as either erroneous or inconclusive, just as mathematics rejects the results of any equation that starts with the proposition that two and two make five. Science has been man's most successful attempt to flee what Carl Sagan called "the demon haunted world" – science *cannot* be used to pave the way back to such primitive madness.

I suppose we can accept it as a compliment to science that agnostics and theists are using it to attempt to resurrect the primitive fantasies inherited from the infancy of our species, but the powerful electricity of modern thought cannot be used to resurrect the Frankenstein of superstitious falsehoods.

Let's look at the "Dimension X" argument in more detail.

Concepts and Instances

A central tenet of rational thinking is to recognize that an *instance* is not a *concept*. A mathematical process such as multiplication is a concept that applies to any general arrangement of numbers; it cannot be called a concept if it only applies to one particular calculation. You need an "x" to have an equation; $16/4=4$ is not an equation, but an instance, a particular application of a general process called division.

In the same way, alternate dimensions cannot be invented that only contain gods, but rather must be a general concept that encompasses everything. The true argument put forward by agnosticism is not that "Dimension X may contain gods," but rather that "nothing true can be said about our reality, because another reality may exist where truth equals falsehood." In other words, the agnostic position is that *any* positive statement *must be* instantly negated by the possibility of an "opposite dimension."

This proposition falls apart at every conceivable level – and even at some that cannot be conceived!

First of all, saying that we cannot make any absolute positive claims about truth is itself an absolute positive claim about truth – i.e. that truth is impossible. If we say that certainty is impossible, then we have to instantly retract that statement, since we are making a certain statement. It very quickly becomes obvious that nothing of any merit or weight can ever be said if the truth is impossible.

In other words, when the agnostic says that we cannot make any absolute claims because the opposite might be true in another universe, the agnostic cannot put forward this claim, because the opposite might be true in another universe.

All con artists operate by affirming a general rule, and then creating an exception for themselves. A thief wants everyone to respect property rights except him; a counterfeiter wants everyone to accept the value of money except him – and a philosophical con man wants everyone to reject truth except for his own propositions.

Don't fall for it, not for a minute!

The moment an agnostic says, "Gods may exist in another dimension," immediately identify the principle behind his statement, which is that no truth can be stated, and apply it to his own statement, thus rendering it invalid.

The Second Self-Contradiction

The moment that we say, "gods may exist in another universe," we are instantly contradicting ourselves, because the word "gods" contains specific knowledge claims – intelligence, omnipotence, immateriality etc. – which *cannot* be applied to a dimension about which we know nothing! To analogize this, imagine that I tell you that I'm going to play you a video of incomprehensible static – and then I insist that I can clearly see the lyrics to "Woolly Bully" scrolling across the screen.

Only one of these claims can be true – if the video is incomprehensible static, then lyrics cannot scroll across the screen – if the lyrics are scrolling across the screen, the video cannot be incomprehensible.

In the same way, if I create Dimension X, and say that we can know nothing about its contents, I then cannot say that gods may exist there, because I am then saying that I know something about the unknowable contents of Dimension X.

I cannot say that I *know* nothing about a particular entity, but that I also know it is green and furry – only one of these statements can be true.

The moment that I say "gods may exist in another dimension," I am making specific knowledge claims about the contents and processes of this other dimension – i.e. that certain entities with specific characteristics may meet the criteria of existence in another dimension of which I admit I know absolutely nothing at all.

The truth of the matter is that we can say *absolutely nothing* about this other dimension; even if we accept that it may exist, which is problematic enough. We cannot claim to have any knowledge about what may or may not constitute existence in this other realm, or what entities may be possible, or what laws of physics may operate, or anything of the sort. Even the existence of this other realm, let alone its contents, cannot be spoken of – all we can propose is that existence may be the same as nonexistence, and invent an imaginary place where this may be possible.

However, even this argument runs into insurmountable logical contradictions.

It would be ridiculous for me to mail you a letter arguing that mail never gets delivered. If I genuinely believe that mail never gets delivered, it would be illogical for me to write you a letter. If I do write you a letter, my argument that mail never gets delivered is instantly invalidated the moment that you receive it.

In the same way, all human communication relies on physical matter of some kind, either text on paper or on a screen, or sound waves in the ear, or touch for Braille, or some other form of physical manipulation. Silence is the absence of sound waves – or at least of a medium such as air or water to carry them. I cannot deny the existence of a medium while using that medium to carry my argument. I cannot rationally yell in your ear that sound does not exist, because I'm relying on the existence of sound to carry my argument.

In the same way, I cannot rationally put forward the argument that all language is meaningless, because I must use language to communicate my argument. If my proposition that language is meaningless is true, then using language to communicate that proposition would be ridiculous – if my argument that language has no meaning is heard and understood – to any degree – then it is automatically invalidated.

To rely on existence to communicate the possibility that existence equals nonexistence is equally foolish. The objective existence of air and air pressure and ears and life and minds is required to speak and hear the argument that existence may equal nonexistence. Furthermore, the rational and predictable properties of all that exists in order to communicate an argument are presumed to be objective, since any communication between human beings requires an acceptance of the objective properties of matter.

For example, if you tell me that gods exist, and I reply, "Yes, I agree that gods do not exist," you will doubtless correct my erroneous feedback on your position. This is only possible if the words have at least some objective meaning, and sound waves do not magically mutate from voice to ears, and so on. For words to be formed, spoken and heard, both existence and nonexistence must be accepted, since all sound waves have peaks and valleys. Text as well must have the presence and absence of somewhat contrasting colours, otherwise only one colour is seen, which is not an argument.

All human communication thus relies on the difference between existence and nonexistence, presence and absence, and accepts as axiomatic the objective behavior of matter and energy, and at least tolerable objectivity in language.

When we understand all this, we understand that using strict and objective differences between existence and nonexistence – as well as accepting the objective behavior of matter and energy – to argue that there may be *no differences* between existence and nonexistence, and that matter and energy may exhibit no objective behavior, is exactly the same as sending a letter claiming that letters are never delivered.

Ah, but perhaps I have misunderstood something! Perhaps I am sending a letter telling you that letters are only *sometimes* not delivered, in which case my argument may be somewhat weakened, but it is not entirely self-contradictory.

The agnostic, after all, does not claim that gods *do* exist in another universe, but rather only that they *may* exist.

However, this is looking at the wrong side of the agnostic argument. The agnostic is making the absolute claim that absolute claims are invalid. "You *cannot* say that gods do not exist, because they may exist in another dimension." This is not a relativistic or sliding scale, but rather an absolute negation. "You cannot say," is the equivalent of "mail is never delivered." It is not the possibility of error that the agnostic is affirming, but rather the impossibility of absolute knowledge claims of any kind. This is an absolute statement that rejects absolutism, which of course renders it invalid.

Agnosticism is one of the rare examples of a truly cosmic fail.

AGNOSTICISM AND PRINCIPLES

Let's look at another argument against agnosticism.

Perhaps you think I am overstating the case – but the agnostic argument is so pervasive, and so ridiculous, that I do not think we can drive enough stakes into its hollow heart.

The agnostic claim that no truth statement can be valid because of a possible opposite universe cannot only apply to gods, but rather must apply to every object in the universe – and every argument as well! Thus, when the agnostic says "gods may exist in another dimension," the "opposite possibility principle" applies *even to his own words*, which can then be rationally reinterpreted, according to his own principles, as the *exact opposite* of what he is saying, i.e. "there can be no other dimensions, and gods cannot exist." If the agnostic protests that this was not his meaning, he can be told that he cannot affirm his meaning in any way, because in this other dimension, his words may have the exact opposite meaning. It is the same principle that he is applying to the atheist, and so he cannot reasonably complain when it boomerangs back and knocks over the foolish house of cards he is pretending to build.

The moment that the agnostic asserts that it is impossible to state with certainty that gods *cannot* exist, due to this possible alternate dimension, then his statement is automatically invalidated as well, since in this alternate dimension, gods may not exist either, or his words may mean the opposite of what he thinks they mean in this dimension, and so on. No sane person can use this other dimension to affirm or deny *any* truth statement in this dimension – and so the agnostic merely takes himself out of the bounds of civilized and rational debate.

The moment an agnostic hears this argument, he will doubtless say, "But..."

However, I merely interrupt him to reply, "You cannot use the word 'but,' since the word 'but' might have the exact opposite meaning in some alternate dimension."

I would continue this process with every word he spoke after that, until he either dropped his position, or my company, which would be a relief either way.

This is what I mean when I say that all con artists wish to create a general rule, with a magical exception for themselves – the agnostic wishes to cast universal doubt on truth statements, except all the ones that *he* happens to make.

AGNOSTICISM AND CONSISTENCY

Since agnosticism is fundamentally an epistemological position, it cannot be confined to the existence of gods, but rather must be fundamental to all forms of human knowledge.

However, I have yet to hear an agnostic argue that we must abolish prisons, since a criminal's guilt can never be established with certainty, since in another dimension, he might not have committed the crime. In Western legal systems, crimes must be proven "beyond a reasonable doubt," but in the agnostic formulation of truth, no such standard can ever be achieved.

This kind of exceptionalism is dully inevitable when dealing with religion. It never applies anywhere else.

To take another example, it is illegal to sell bogus cures for real illnesses – however, not only is Christianity's "cure" utterly unproven, but even the "illness" itself – sin – is completely invented. Can we imagine a priest being hauled before a court for fraud, for selling a nonsense cure to an invented disease? If not, why not?

We also have laws against hate speech, or the incitement of hatred against particular groups. However, the Bible commands believers to kill gays, atheists, sorcerers, heretics, disobedient children and witches and just about everyone else who draws breath. A comic in Canada was recently hauled before the human rights commission for making a joke about homosexuals – can we imagine the printers and distributors of the Bible being charged in such a manner? If not, why not?

Gods and Non-Existence?

Even if we accept the opposite-planet Bizarro world of the agnostic position – and even if we accept that knowledge claims can be made about an unknowable realm, the agnostic position still falls flat.

There are only two possibilities for our future relationship with Dimension X – either we will *never* interact with it in any way, or we will find some way to penetrate its mysteries. In the first case, Dimension X will never be discovered, in which case it is merely "nonexistence" with a silly alias, and cannot be used to reject any knowledge claims. Since it remains a mere synonym for nonexistence, it cannot be used to reject nonexistence. In this case, an agnostic cannot say, "I reject that gods cannot exist by defining nonexistence as synonymous with existence – just calling it 'Dimension X' for funsies."

Ah, but perhaps someday we will find a way to send a probe into Dimension X, and record some of its properties. In this case, we will be translating Dimension X into something that exists here, in our universe, just as a spectrograph translates light into waves. In other words, Dimension X will have to show up somewhere, somehow in our universe to confirm its existence, and can no longer be used as a synonym for nonexistence.

Alternatively, if Zeus is currently doing cartwheels in Dimension X, he might trip and stick his finger through the time-space continuum and poke a hole in our moon. In this case, we would have objective and empirical evidence for this event, which would constitute proof that something rather extraordinary had occurred.

In other words, the properties and characteristics of Dimension X will have to be translated into something that exists in *this* universe in order to confirm its existence and record its properties. If Dimension X never has any impact on our universe, then it is completely synonymous with nonexistence, and can never be used to reject nonexistence. Using the standard of nonexistence to reject nonexistence is entirely self-contradictory, the equivalent of saying "I reject the nonexistence of X by accepting that it does not exist, but using a different word." If a surgeon said that a dead patient still lived because he used the word "gool" to mean "dead," we would not accept his argument as particularly rational. The agnostic claim that gods cannot be said to not exist because one can use the phrase "dimension x" as a synonym for nonexistence is equally foolish and irrational.

Gods and the Supernatural

That which is self-contradictory cannot exist. Gods are self-contradictory entities. Therefore gods cannot exist.

What if a god is invented which does not possess self-contradictory characteristics?

Ah, then it is not a god.

We can imagine that 21st century man would appear godlike to our Stone Age ancestors – however, the sane among us do not believe that we have become gods due to our advanced technology.

In the same way, we may meet among the stars fantastically advanced beings – however they will not be gods, but rather just highly evolved life forms. We may meet telepathic beings who can travel through time and have made themselves immortal, but we will never meet carbon-based lifeforms that can live on the surface of the sun, or Oompa-Loompas who live in a square circle, are composed of both fire and ice, and can go North and South at the same time.

Thus it is axiomatic that gods cannot exist – if they are gods, then they cannot exist; if they exist, then they are not gods.

Accidental Knowledge?

Imagine that archaeologists come across some squiggly prehistoric cave painting that, when viewed at a certain angle, has vague similarities to the equation "E=mc²".

Would this overthrow our entire sense of causality and the evolution of knowledge? Would we imagine that a primitive caveman largely incapable of language or mathematics had somehow discovered one of the most complex and challenging equations of modern physics?

Of course not.

We would smile at the strange coincidence, but would no more imagine a Stone Age genius physicist then we would grant a doctorate to the wind, should it happen to blow a series of sand dunes into a similar equation.

In other words, the effects of knowledge cannot exist prior to that knowledge. I could probably teach my infant daughter to scratch out "$E=mc^2$," but I would not imagine that she understood any of its reasoning, evidence or contents. A sick animal might break into a pharmacy and eat the pills that co-incidently happened to treat its illness, but we would not call such an animal a pharmacist or a doctor.

Almost all of our conceptions of deities have come down to us from the past — and generally the pre-scientific past. When we consider the 10,000 or so gods that human beings have believed in at one time or another, we clearly understand that the development and depiction of these gods was not based on any scientific or rational understanding of the universe. Even if the impossible actually occurred, and some being were found somewhere in the universe that closely matched the description of some ancient deity, this would not be proof that such a god existed in the past, and was the source of that knowledge. Either this would be mere coincidence, or we would have to accept the reality that such a being visited our ancestors, who recorded his actual presence, which is not proof of the existence of a god, but rather a tourist.

Any historical knowledge claim about deities existed prior to any empirical evidence or proof, and thus remains in the realm of pure fantasy. Even if evidence were to accumulate at some point in the future, this does not grant prescience to the accidental imaginings of past ages. In other words, the hope that some theists and agnostics have that proofs for gods will be found in the future does not validate any *existing* claims about the natures and properties of deities. All prior and existing claims of knowledge about gods are false, regardless of what shows up in the future, in this or any other dimension.

DEITIES BEFORE TIME?

Some theists – and even agnostics – use the same "Dimension X" argument examined above, but place the alternate universe in a time *before* our own, rather than parallel to it in some manner.

This does not fundamentally change any of the arguments – either this universe before our own will never have any impact on us, in which case it is just another word for nonexistence, or it will, in which case it will be empirically measurable within our own universe, and subject to all the same laws of physics as everything else we examine. In other words, once it enters into our universe, it cannot contain self-contradictory properties, and therefore cannot be a god.

QUANTUM PHYSICS

Quantum physics is the latest in a long line of scientific bags that people like to dump their crazy, pseudo-scientific ideas in to. The admitted strangeness and apparent self-contradictory behavior of subatomic particles is sometimes enlisted as yet another "alternate realm" wherein gods might exist.

The frank reality of quantum effects is that they have no impact whatsoever upon sense perception, since any and all quantum effects cancel each other out long before the aggregation of particles is perceptible by our unaided senses. This is why an electron may seem to be in two places at the same time, but a table never is.

Clearly, life cannot exist at a subatomic level, which is why we never think of a proton as alive, even if it is contained within a living being. Since a deity must be alive – at least in some sense of the word – it cannot exist at the subatomic level, since even the simplest form of life is a highly complex aggregation of cells and energy.

Furthermore, since the individual subatomic particles examined by quantum physics can never have any effect on objects perceivable by our senses, this invalidates all historical – i.e. prior to quantum physics – conceptions of deities. Finding *ex post facto* homes for gods in quantum physics, when all concepts of deities evolved *prior* to any knowledge of quantum physics – is a ridiculous and desperate attempt to rescue the irrational through an appeal to the scientific.

HARM TO CHILDREN?

It has long been accepted by rational thinkers that religion occupies a magically aggressive place in the pantheon of human thought, remaining strangely impervious to the rational standards that have long since felled other superstitions.

As Richard Dawkins has pointed out, every religious person is virtually a complete atheist, in that he rejects the existence of every other God but the one he worships.

To understand this more clearly, imagine a mathematics tutor named Bob who refused to teach any strict methodology for solving problems.

If you were to hire Bob, and your child were to correctly answer the problem of 3x3, Bob would have to reply that it was impossible to say that three times three make nine, because in an alternate universe they might make the opposite of nine. Bob would further instruct your child not to answer any question with any certainty, and always to include this caveat with regards to any and all forms of knowledge. Bob would also say that none of his instructions — even that one — can be accepted as true, because they might be false in another universe.

Thus, when responding to a roll call at school, your son cannot say that he is present, because in another universe, he might be absent. Furthermore, he cannot actually go to school, because in another universe, the school might be located in the opposite direction from his house. He cannot go to bed, because in another universe, it might be an alligator. He cannot eat vegetables, because in another universe, they might be poison – and so on…

Surely we would view such a tutor as a sworn enemy to the mental health of our child, and would be horrified at the inevitable results of his bizarre philosophy, and would have to spend a good deal of time unravelling the Gordian knot of impossible contradictions he had tied our child's mind into.

Principles which claim universality, but which cannot conceivably be universalized, are self-contradictory and false by definition.

Agnosticism and Religion

While agnosticism generally refrains from attacking specific positive claims about the nature of deities (other than to say that they may exist in another dimension defined as synonymous with nonexistence), religions are entirely founded on making positive and universal claims about the nature, intentions, personalities, morals and properties of deities.

An agnostic will say that an invisible man might live in the boarded-up house next door; a priest will tell you everything that the invisible man thinks and wants and is capable of.

Agnosticism and religion both require the substitution of socially-acceptable synonyms for falsehood in order to affirm their invalid positions.

Agnostics substitute "other dimensions" for "nonexistence," while theists substitute "faith" for "falsehood."

Why is faith false?

Well, as the Latin phrase has it – *Credo quia absurdum* ("I believe because it is absurd"). A square circle is an impossible entity, and therefore cannot exist. We do not have to hunt the entire universe from edge to edge to know that a square circle does not exist; it is not an act of will to accept that a square circle does not exist, it is simply a recognition of reality and the nature of existence.

A square circle is an absurd concept – or rather, to be more accurate, it is an *anti*-concept, in that it takes two valid but incompatible concepts and crashes them together to create a crazy mishmash of impossibility.

Take any property or ethic of the Christian God – to just pick on one absurd anti-concept – and the contradictory nature is clear.

- "That which exists must have been created, but God, who exists, was never created."
- "God is all-knowing and all-powerful, which are both impossible."
- "God punishes a man for actions which are predetermined."
- "God punishes rebellious angels, although their rebellion was completely predetermined."
- "God claims to be morally perfect, although God fails the test of most of his 10 Commandments."
- Etc.

For any religion that involves prayer or supplication to be valid, the following steps must all be rationally validated and empirically proven:

1. A deity must exist (call him "Jeb").
2. Jeb must have the interest and power to interfere in the universe.
3. Jeb must have the interest and willingness to interfere in human affairs.
4. Jeb must listen to prayers, rather than just read minds.
5. Jeb must only listen to prayers from the members of a particular sect.
6. Jeb must monitor and record good and bad behavior.
7. Ideally, Jeb must punish the members of alternate sects, or those who pray in an incorrect or inconsistent fashion.
8. Jeb must also not reward those who do not give money to his priests – and ideally, punish said folks.

As we can see, since even the existence of a deity is conceptually ridiculous, not even the first domino in this increasingly absurd row falls down.

In other words, the propositions of religion do not "require faith," but rather are simply *false* – and as a result, since they command obedience and money, they are exploitative, abusive and destructive.

Religion as Child Abuse?

In his recent book "God Is Not Great," Christopher Hitchens asked whether religion was child abuse, but in my view did not provide a very satisfactory answer. The question can be easily resolved through the philosophical approach of *universalization*.

It is generally accepted in society that children are mentally deficient – and in some ways, of course, they are, in language acquisition and the processing of consequences to actions and so on.

It is generally considered acceptable in a religious society to teach children that God will reward them for obedience to their elders, and punish them for disobedience.

However, we cannot put only *children* into the category of "mentally deficient," since there are those with impaired mental faculties either due to a physical brain problem or injury, or due to age- or illness-related deterioration.

Let us take the example of mentally challenged individuals with Down's syndrome.

Imagine that a home for such individuals existed, run by a man named Bob. Every morning, Bob reminds his bewildered and mentally challenged wards that the air is full of invisible demons who will attack their brains, eyes, teeth and tongues if they *ever* disobey one of Bob's Commandments. Even if they are slow to obey, these demons will attack them in their dreams, and suck out their life essence, and spit it into a lake of fire, where it will burn for eternity. Every morning, they must get on their knees and plead for Bob's good opinion, otherwise he might butcher all of them by drowning them in toilets, as he did once before when he was offended…

We could go on and on, but I think that we all understand that this would be verbal and emotional abuse of the very worst and most destructive kind. The traumatized mentally challenged victims of such a nightmare environment would not be able to differentiate Bob's terrifying tales from actual reality, and would live in abject terror, and we would consider it a staggeringly evil abuse of power for Bob to verbally attack and mentally infect his victims in such a manner.

It's hard to imagine that we would judge the situation any differently if Bob ran a home for elderly adults with dementia, and terrified old ladies in the same manner. In either case, we would view Bob as a deranged sadist, lacking any shred of human compassion for his victims, and our hearts would go out to the suffering that he was inflicting through the vengeful power of his demonic language.

(As a minor tangent, this argument is exactly the same for spanking – would we accept it as morally valid to spank the elderly for their forgetfulness?)

Is religion child abuse?

Yes, if it is false. As it is.

Mentally challenged individuals with Down's Syndrome – as well as most elderly people – are nowhere near as vulnerable as children, since most of them have adults taking a significant interest in their long-term well-being.

However, when parents inflict demonic and terrifying tales of religious superstition on the tender, trusting and dependent minds of their children, who will intervene to save them?

Sadly, only real philosophers, for the rest of the intellectual classes are too busy inventing hiding places for the gods to intervene and save the children.

POWER OR VIRTUE? A LOVE STORY

Almost all deities are objects of worship, but it is hard to know with any certainty exactly what is being worshiped. Certainly gods are very powerful – infinitely powerful, in most formulations – but I have never met a religious person who worships only the power of his God. No, it is always the *virtue* of God that is worshiped; the power is merely incidental.

However, the virtue of a deity is problematic on many levels.

If human beings only ever wanted to eat the food that was best for them, we would have no need for the science of nutrition. Our desire for fats and sugars drives the need for nutritional information and discipline, just as our desire for energy conservation drives the need for information about exercise. If we could all automatically do any mathematical calculation in our heads, we would not need to be taught mathematics, and so on.

All human disciplines thus arise to counter desires which run against our best long-term interests. The balancing of long and short-term interests is the very essence of wisdom – the short-term hit of a cigarette versus the long-term risk of lung cancer, the short-term emotional relief of verbal abuse versus the long-term harm to our relationships, to name just two examples.

The discipline of *ethics* is no different.

The need for virtue in humanity arises out of mortality, and weakness, and temptation, and relative powerlessness – none of which concerns God in any way. Would God need to be courageous, if He was all-powerful? It's hard to see how. Would He need to remind himself to be honest, if He could suffer no negative consequences for his honesty? Would He find it challenging to resist the temptations of peer pressure? He is peerless, of course!

In many video games, there is a secret "god mode," which allows players to stroll through the game without taking any damage from enemies, usually with infinite ammunition and pixel-shredding weapons. I can't imagine thinking that a player was really good if he completed a game in "God mode" – in fact, I can't imagine why he would bother. In the same vein, if Mike Tyson in his prime were to jump into a boxing ring with a five-year-old girl, and beat her senseless, it would be hard to admire his athletic prowess.

Can we admire the virtue of a being who has no need for virtue? That would be like admiring someone for not smoking, though he had never been exposed to cigarettes, or praising the sensible fish-based diet followed by a man marooned on a desert island.

Worshiping a God for His virtue is like admiring a man in a coma for refraining from alcoholism.

God and Virtue?

Even if we put all of this aside, the question still remains: how do we know that God is virtuous?

If we are at all interested in efficiency – and as mortal beings it must have some interest to us – the first place we look for virtue is *consistency with stated principles*. This does not automatically prove virtue, since those stated principles might be immoral – but it does mean that we can at least check for hypocrisy before venturing further.

Thus integrity is a necessary – but not sufficient – criterion for virtue.

If we want to lose weight, and go to a bookstore, and see 50 diet books on the shelf, how likely are we to choose the diet book written by a fat author? Would such a book not more properly belong in the comedy section? "Ah," you may say, "but the fact that an author is fat does not automatically invalidate his diet." That is certainly true, but so what? Life is short, decisions are endless, and we cannot investigate every conceivable claim. It is enough to know that a fat dietitian either *is* following his own diet, in which case it will be unlikely to help us lose weight, or he is promoting a diet that he himself does not follow, which calls his judgment into question, to say the least. Either way, we move on.

The same principle applies to ethics.

If a man constantly preaches the virtue of helping others in need, and then steps over a man bleeding to death in a gutter, we cannot reasonably praise his integrity. While we may agree with him that helping others in need is morally good, his actions inform us that *he* does not agree with his own moral arguments.

Most religions explicitly state that helping others in need is morally good – think of the parable of the Good Samaritan in the New Testament. However, since gods do not exist, and so cannot intervene, religions have the rather challenging task of explaining why their "moral" God does not help those in need. If it is immoral for travelers on the road to ignore a bleeding man, when it will cost them both time and resources to help him, is it not infinitely more immoral for God to refrain from helping, when it will cost God neither time nor resources, since He has an infinity of both?

We could go on *ad nauseum* with these examples, such as the genocidal habits of the Old Testament deity, contrasted with His commandment "Thou Shalt Not Kill," but I'm sure you get the general point.

If we are wise, we do not take a man's claim that he is virtuous at face value, but will ask first about the *contents* of his moral beliefs, and then about his practical consistency with those values. A man can only be considered virtuous when he has good values, and strives for and achieves reasonable consistency with those values. If he has bad values, clearly he cannot be virtuous, just as if he has good values but does not act on them.

Gods command men to fight evil, but gods allow evil in the world. Gods prohibit killing, but gods kill. Gods command their followers not to judge others, but gods judge. Gods punish the predetermined actions of people, which shows about as much maturity and wisdom as jailing a cell phone. Gods continually act in direct contradiction to their own stated moral values, which is a hallmark of great *immorality*.

A man raised by wolves who has no conception of ethics may be forgiven for stealing; a man who preaches respect for property is fully responsible if he steals, because he has already displayed his knowledge of ethics. We would not fault a waiter for failing to perform an emergency tracheotomy; a doctor would far more responsible, since he possesses the necessary knowledge to help.

Thus it is hard to understand exactly what is being worshiped when a God is being praised. Is it power? But power is morally neutral at best, and while it may elicit awe or deference, it cannot be morally worshiped in and of itself. Is it virtue? But we have only the God's *word* that He is virtuous, which is exactly what would we would expect from a hypocritical con artist bent on praising himself only to arouse admiration and obedience in us.

The whole question of virtue gets buried under the contradictory kaleido-scope of justifications for religion. Theists are faced with the impossible task of attempting to justify primitive and brutal superstitions according to mod-ern moral and scientific sensibilities. The more intelligent among them know that this is impossible, so they create a bewildering miasma of contradictions, foggy stall tactics, bizarre combinations of moral relativism for adults ("this passage is metaphorical") and abusive absolutism for children ("Jesus died for your sins!").

The Costs of False Ethics

Our acceptance of these tactics – which would be laughed out of the room in any other human discipline – has come at a truly catastrophic cost to our moral development and understanding as a species.

Over the past 2,500 years, we have advanced in almost every human discipline – *except* ethics.

Despite our staggering advances in technology, medicine, physics, biology, engineering – and almost any other field you would care to name – our progress in moral philosophy has not changed since the days – and death – of Socrates.

We still have wars, and torture, and child abuse, and national debts, and the forced indoctrination of the young – and we cannot come to any moral standards that can be generally accepted by reasonably intelligent people the world over. We despise theft, and then accept taxes – we despise murder, and praise soldiers – we tell our children not to use force, and then we use government force to 'educate' them.

The original formulation of ethics was to create a set of rules, to encourage people to follow those rules – even if they did not understand them – and to punish transgressors with imprisonment and fines in the here and now, and eternal damnation in the hereafter.

The threat of secular retribution from the state, combined with the hope for internal guilt and self attack from religion, was the best that could be achieved when humanity was still convinced that the Earth was flat, trees had souls and the world rested on an infinity of giant turtles.

Nothing has changed in any fundamental way since the dawn of thought. We still encourage people to be "good" by following social standards and mostly arbitrary laws, and then violently attack them when they break the obviously arbitrary rules that have been invented.

To take a simple example, to kill a man in the street is a great moral crime; to kill a man on a battlefield is a great moral virtue. "No green costume" equals moral evil – "green costume" equals moral heroism. If one man tells you to murder, you get a jail cell – if another man tells you to murder, you get medals and a pension.

Alternatively, the initiation of force against a peaceful individual for the purpose of removing his property is clearly theft when done in a dark alley; the taxation policies of a great nation are, as the saying goes, "the price we pay to live in a civilized society."

I cannot lock my neighbor in my basement for making too much noise, but I can call the police to lock him in jail if he grows certain vegetables in his basement, which has far less effect on me.

If I am poor, and I steal food, I go to jail – however, if I vote for politicians to forcibly transfer other people's wealth to me through the welfare state, I am an engaged citizen.

These are all paradoxes that every reasonably intelligent person has mulled over at one time or another, but they have remained essentially unchanged for thousands of years, and I would argue that this is largely due to religion.

A false answer – particularly when it is highly profitable to liars – is the ultimate barrier to progress in human thought. Religion is the worst possible answer to the question of ethics, since it is not an answer at all, but merely a threat based on falsehoods.

One of the reasons that medieval economics remained so primitive and unproductive was the Guild system, which required many years of poorly paid labor to learn even the most simple and menial of tasks. Those who had already passed through the system made more money individually than they would have if the system had been suddenly abandoned, and free competition had opened up. The older and wealthier members of society thus continued to block free competition from the young, and while they may have maintained their own income in the short run, they killed economic growth in the long run, which was to their own detriment, and the detriment of their children of course.

The threat was punishment from the state, the lie was that seven years of apprenticeship were necessary to become, say, a bricklayer – and so society stagnated at near starvation levels for almost a thousand years, until the shortage of labor that arose from the Black Death began to unravel the Guild system.

In the same way, the "moral teaching" of religion is only a threat – secular punishment from the state, eternal punishment from God – based on a series of lies, i.e. that gods exist, are moral, and must be obeyed.

The institutionalization and profitable exploitation of this system has effectively barred philosophers from examining morality from a rational and secular standpoint. Either philosophers are religious (or afraid of the religious), in which case they tend to avoid attacking fundamental moral problems, for fear of arousing attack – or philosophers are statists (or afraid of the government), in which case they tend to avoid attacking fundamental moral problems, for fear of arousing attack.

Those who work for churches would view any rational system of secular ethics as a direct threat to their income and position, the same goes for those who work for the state.

Thus "right-wingers" tend to be more in favor of a smaller state, but are very religious; "left-wingers" tend to be more skeptical of religion and secular in nature, but tend to be more in favor of a larger state.

"Choose your poison" seems to be our only approach to solving moral problems.

Any society which relies on false and contradictory morality – and all societies currently fall into this category – must substitute aggression for argument in the instruction of children. A child who asks why a soldier gets a medal for killing in a war, when he would be thrown in jail in peacetime, can receive no sane and rational answer, for none exists. Parents, priests and teachers seem to be fundamentally averse to saying that they do not know the answer to this question, or any of the other hundreds of ethical questions posed by children.

Because we do not know the answer to these questions, we must threaten children in order to throw them off the scent, so to speak. This may be overt, or more subtle, through exasperated sighs, rolling one's eyes, and rolling out the tired old bromide that the child will understand when he gets older.

False moral principles are the foundation for the greatest edifices of human society – the state, the military, the police, the church, public schools and so on. Since these enormous and powerful institutions rest on ridiculous and indefensible moral contradictions, to persist in questioning these principles is to take an axe to the base of the tree of the world. The entire profit and sense of human society sits like an enormous inverted pyramid on a few shaky and trembling – and false – ethical axioms.

Our lack of progress in solving moral problems without using aggression is entirely attributable to the confusing infections of religiosity. Just as it took a secular mind to solve the problem of biological evolution, it will take a secular mind to solve the problem of secular, rational and scientific ethics. However, any theory that defers to religion must inevitably create a central vortex of wild irrationality that it must skip around, distorting and ruining the theory as a whole.

In the same way, any theory that defers to statism, taxation and war creates exactly the same vortex, since it cannot ban the initiation of force to solve social problems, yet it must ban the initiation of force to solve personal problems, and so mealy-mouthed madness can only follow from such dismal and initial compromises. "The initiation of force through taxation is moral, but the initiation of force through theft is immoral…" "The initiation of force in war is moral, the initiation of force without war is immoral…" "Public violence is good, private violence is bad…" etc.

This is why the modern coterie of secular atheists will never be able to solve the problem of ethics, since they remain wedded to the state – to the initiation of force – as a central moral axiom within society. Thus Sam Harris says that we need to solve the problem of war by creating a world government, while Richard Dawkins remains fundamentally unable to criticize the state, since he is fundamentally an employee of the state, while Christopher Hitchens is still recovering from his totalitarian Marxist impulses, and continues to praise the obviously unjust and immoral Iraq war (though in charity we can safely assume that results more from his family military history than any objective judgement).

It seems enormously difficult to overcome our own prejudices, and the historical errors that seem almost to have been embedded into our very DNA. It may be too much to ask for true originality in solving these problems, but we should at the very least ask for an avoidance of the false answers that have so repetitively failed for the past 2,500 years.

We may not yet know the right way to go, but we should at least stop going in the wrong direction.

Why Gods?

It is helpful, but not essential, for atheism to explain why the concept of gods is so widespread and prevalent among mankind. The 10,000 or so gods that lie scattered across the past and present cultures of our species must represent some form of universal content or meaning for this fantasy to be so widespread.

In general, religion has gone through four major phases — the first was *animism*, or the idea that every rock and leaf and tree was imbued with a spiritual force. In this approach, a farmer would profusely apologize to a rock before moving it out of the way of his plow. It is fairly easy to understand that this arose from a fundamental confusion between what is living and what is not, or what has consciousness, and what does not. A man who thinks that a rock deserves an apology lives in an extremely primitive state of mind, wherein the division between his own consciousness and inanimate matter has not yet been established. My 18 month old daughter is losing the habit of saying hello to the toilet, and her bath, and her toes, which gives you a sense of how primitive this phase is.

In the second phase of religion, the distinction between living and not living becomes established, and a multiplicity of deities that are specifically and thoroughly anthropomorphic take refuge somewhere above the clouds, or on the peak of a mountain, sucking up in their wake all of the projected consciousness that formerly resided in rocks and trees and rivers. This is a vast improvement in accuracy – not to mention sanity – in that the differentiation between conscious and unconscious becomes established in a much wider sphere.

In the third phase, the warring multiplicity of gods is in a sense hunted down, rounded up and herded into one big squirming bag of pseudo-monotheism. The former glorious ribaldry of the ancient Greek religions becomes diluted and caged into a tyrannical hierarchy of a single, inhuman and utterly abstract God. This phase contains a variety of insurmountable tensions, which inevitably fragment the new monotheism into an even more bizarre version of the older polytheism, such as the Holy Trinity and the thousands of saints.

In the fourth phase, religion becomes a set of more or less convincing fairy tales, wherein obedience to a complete text is not required, but followers can pick and choose what they like, according to their own personal preferences and tastes, and God is turned into a sort of ideological lapdog, which trails after the prejudices of the believer, imbuing his own personal bigotries with a vague glow of eternal approval.

In all these phases, there is a deep and consistent sense of a vast and powerful consciousness that lies outside the range of our conscious ego, which contains deep and mysterious elements of eternity; which existed before us, and will continue to exist after us, which informs and guides many if not most of our decisions, reveals its purposes and intentions through visions and dreams, frustrates our vices and supports our virtues, and responds indirectly and metaphorically to abasement and supplication.

It is scarcely a novel insight to point out that our minds are divided between our conscious ego and our subconscious. Our conscious ego needs little explanation; it is the self aware part of us that responds to willpower, focus, attention, and has direct access to the memories that we have accumulated in our lifetimes. It is a precise and astoundingly powerful tool that in a very real sense can be called the most mortal part of ourselves, since it grows and develops with us, and will certainly die with us, as will all of our personal memories.

However, there exists below consciousness, or surrounding consciousness, the *subconscious*, whose processing power dwarfs the puny efforts of our conscious mind, and which also contains an element of eternity within itself. Our conscious memories are specific to our own lives, as are our more conscious choices and plans. I may dream at night of something I experienced that day, but the capacity for the experience of dreaming is not something that I have chosen, but rather something that my subconscious mind has developed and inherited and refined over millions of years.

The subconscious mind, which controls everything from our heart rate to our breathing to the increasing uneasiness we experience when in a dangerous situation we have not yet noticed consciously, is like an eternal guardian angel – or avenging devil if we have done evil – which is constantly prodding us with interfering emotions and sensations, discouraging us with fear and guilt, spurring us on with desire and pleasure, lecturing us about our choices in nightly dreams, whipping us on with short-term lust while simultaneously cautioning us with fears about the long-term stability of our sexual partners – to name just a few.

When we think of religion, we think of a puny consciousness – that of man – embedded in an eternal, infinite and seemingly omniscient consciousness which never shows itself directly, but which takes an enormous interest in us, and evaluates our choices and preferences, and rewards us and punishes us, and responds in maddeningly oblique ways to our direct and painful supplications.

Gods are also experienced as existing before us, and living on after us, which directly relates to the quasi-eternal nature of the subconscious, which existed prior to our conscious mind and memories even in the individual, and which is the ancient foundation upon which the temple of our ego was built.

The mind of God is also considered to be vastly superior to that of man – is this not also an exact description of the subconscious, whose processing power has been estimated as 7,000 times that of the conscious mind?

Man is considered to be a creation of God, and God is a deep and eternal consciousness that has existed forever – is this not an exact description of the relationship between the conscious ego and the subconscious? As a species, and in our own lives, our ego evolves out of our subconscious, which is why we cannot remember our very early years. I have an arm which I can call my arm in a sense, but it is not really my arm, because it existed before I experienced an "I." My arm preceded me, since it developed in the womb – and my ego had no part in its planning or creation, but rather my ego grew out of my body, many years later. My arm, my body and my subconscious existed before me, and certainly my body will exist after me, though my ego will not be around to watch it decompose.

Thus when we say that man is created by God, what we really mean is that the ego is created by the body, which precedes the ego both individually and collectively. My arm preceded my consciousness by years, and human arms in general preceded my particular arm by millions of years. It is in this sense that we are in fact created by an eternal pattern that precedes us, however primitively we may have anthropomorphized this basic truth.

The subconscious – like monotheism – also resists the imposition of a singular identity, no matter how fervently desired. The subconscious contains a vast multiplicity of alter egos, various aspects of the conscious mind designed to fit into whatever hierarchy wraps around us in the moment – as well as the multiple alter egos of those around us, those who raised us and taught us and, perhaps, harmed and abused us.

To take an obvious example, when I was a child I had a teacher who was a bully, and this teacher would immediately become servile when the principal came into the classroom – I have within my subconscious not only this teacher as an individual, but this teacher as a personality with multiple alter egos. I have my own alter egos, as well at the alter egos of thousands of other people I have met over the course of my life, which is why, since religion is merely a superstitious description of our subconscious, monotheism can never hold.

Things which do not work generally do not last, which is why few of us indulge in rain dances anymore when we really want a downpour. There is something in religion, though, which *does* work, despite its obvious falsehoods, and my argument is that what works is the act of asking a superior intelligence for guidance and wisdom. The simple fact is that people who pray often *do* experience a response, and the obvious and empirical answer is that they are asking for wisdom from their own subconscious, which responds in its usual oblique yet amazingly accurate fashion. A man who asks God for an answer is asking his subconscious for advice, and anyone who has spent any significant time on the couch of a good therapist, examining his dreams and his feelings and his impulses, sooner or later understands the power, fertility and objectivity of the subconscious – and once this is understood, the accuracy and utility of religion is revealed. The clarity and precision of the conscious mind requires no explanation, since we experience it countless times every day – the wisdom and astounding parallel processing power of the subconscious is largely only available to those who approach it on bended knee, with humility and patience and bottomless curiosity.

This is not to say, however, that religion is a form of self-knowledge, or that grandiose superstitions are somehow equivalent to humble introspection. It is certainly true that among those already predisposed to gentleness, virtue and courage, the impulses returned from the subconscious can truly aid them in achieving and maintaining these admirable virtues – but as we all know, these are not the only kinds of people in the world. I get many messages from religious people who tell me that although I am not a believer, their God loves me. While I certainly do appreciate these warm sentiments, I cannot afford to take them very seriously, because what would I say if they wrote to tell me that their God hated me for my unbelief, as the Bible says? If I accept irrational love, I cannot very well reject irrational hatred. There is an enormous difference between humbly consulting wise but hard to access aspects of myself, and believing that I am receiving divine commandments from a perfect and all-powerful intelligence outside myself.

The essence of self-knowledge is *negotiation*, the recognition that every aspect of the self has a valid seat at the table, and deserves to be heard, but that none shall rule. Some people think of this as a democracy of the self, but I think that is a tragically inaccurate and destructive way to look at it, because in a democracy, the government always has the final say, and enforces its will through the force of law. It is infinitely more accurate and healthy to say that what is required is a stateless state of mind, or the anarchy of the self, where all is negotiation, and no final arbiter can enforce decisions. The discomfort generated by refusing to promote an inner dictator – even temporarily – to a position of final authority can be extreme, particularly since we are raised in such horribly authoritarian structures – school, church, so often the family – yet it is necessary for us to progress as a species to a more peaceful world.

The closest current analogy to the anarchy of self is the voluntarism of free-market, without government, where wealth and authority may ebb and flow, but all is negotiation and peaceful interaction.

Religion supports the promotion of the subconscious to a position of ultimate and final authority, since it worships the subconscious as a God, which is extremely dangerous, since no aspect of the self should ever be a tyrant in the mind of a healthy man, just as no single muscle in the body should dominate all other muscles. We require a highly complex interplay of hundreds of muscles even to walk – when one muscle becomes dominant, we call that a cramp, and consider it an extremely uncomfortable situation that needs to be alleviated at once.

In more extreme cases, a man who prays to an imaginary being will hear voices in his head telling him what to do, and religion supports the idea that these voices come from a god, not a horribly damaged part of his own psyche, with all the resulting disasters that can occur from such a tragic misapprehension. It is true that the more gentle among the religious reject the theological validity of those who claim to hear voices coming from God, yet they are on a slippery slope when they take such a noble stand, since if they perceive their contemporaries to be mentally ill for hearing voices and believing in gods, what are they to make of those who wrote their holy texts? Few modern Christians would kneel before a man claiming to be the reincarnation of Jesus Christ, but rather would suggest that he would benefit from the services of a mental health practitioner – would they say the same to Jesus himself? Most Christians would say that Jesus performed miracles, but there is no evidence for this of course, other than the hearsay of other people who were doubtless equally mentally ill. If I said that Christians should worship a friend of mine because he performed miracles that only I could see, would they agree? It is impossible to imagine that they would.

The religious also believe that gods watch and judge us, and this seems entirely in accordance with the subconscious reality of a conscience. A conscience is nothing terribly complex; it is simply the extrapolation of our stated principles into universals, followed by the comparison of our actions to these universals. If I hit my daughter while telling her not to hit others, this basic contradiction – or perhaps more accurately revolting hypocrisy – is instantly noted and retained by my subconscious. I will as a result distinctly feel that there is something wrong with what I am doing, which will either propel me to examine my own hypocrisy, or redouble my attacks upon my daughter for her imagined transgressions.

If I act on impulse, and then invent endless *ex post facto* justifications for my actions, with reference to universal principles, then I become a bewildering, dangerous and annoying hypocrite to those around me. I cannot act with any integrity, because I have erected high and thorny walls between the various aspects of myself that need to come together so that I can act with reasonable consistency.

Unfortunately, philosophy emerged from religion in much the same way that mankind evolved from fetid swamp dwellers, with the result that principles were invented to excuse evil and elevate hypocrisy to the status of virtue. For instance, the Bible commands believers to refrain from murder, but the god considered to be all virtuous kills virtually the entire world in a fit of rage. This kind of staggering hypocrisy requires a vast amount of verbal fencing and befogging to avoid. Rationalizing the irrational was the original basis of philosophy, which is why to create a philosophy based on reason and evidence is such a radical project.

Agnosticism and Cowardice

I **have often** argued that agnostics are cowards, and I would like to make that case here.

First of all, I do not consider the position *itself* to be cowardly, but rather if superior and irrefutable strong atheist arguments are consistently rejected in favor of the mental fog of agnosticism, I consider that cowardly and enormously destructive.

We cannot be reasonably criticized for not adhering to knowledge we have yet to learn. Was an 18th-century physician negligent for failing to prescribe a cure that had not yet been invented? Of course not – but we would condemn a 21st-century physician for such malpractice. I would not criticize my 18 month old daughter for deliberately pouring juice on the carpet, an act I would consider wilfully aggressive on the part of an adult guest.

Thus if you are an agnostic, but have not yet heard the arguments in this book, please do not think that I am calling you a coward – if that even means anything to you – but after you have heard these arguments, if you cannot refute them, and still cling to your irrational position, then that is certainly the label I will apply to you, since you will have earned it.

The basic tenet of agnosticism is that no positive statements about truth can be made because some contradictory evidence may exist in this or some other universe. There is so much that is wrong with this position that it is hard to know even where to start, so let's start with something quite simple, and then work up to the more complex objections.

First of all, agnosticism is always and forever specific only to the existence of deities. I have never once heard an agnostic argue that we cannot call rape wrong because it might be right in some other universe. I recently had a debate on agnosticism with a staunch antigovernment libertarian, who argued that we could not say there were no gods because gods might exist in some other universe. I then asked him how he could assert that governments were immoral, because they might be moral in some other universe? He replied that governments have specific properties, which I did not particularly understand, and I replied that gods also have specific properties, which is why we use the word "gods" rather than "spoon," or "aglet," or "spork," or "tine." He did not respond to this, but I think the point is very clear. If the possible existence of alternate universes where truth equals falsehood invalidates any positive declaration of truth, then this applies *universally*, and not specifically only to gods. I have never heard an agnostic argue for the potential existence of Santa Claus in some other universe, or leprechauns, or square circles, or two and two making five. I have never seen a scientist rejecting the claim that the world is round because in another universe, it might be shaped like a banana.

We can all imagine how offensive it would be for a man to argue that we cannot call rape immoral, or attempt to prevent and punish it, because it might be virtuous in some other dimension – such a man would be obviously attempting to deal with his own psychological problems by creating some nonsensical and fogging philosophical junkyard of confusion. Have you ever heard an agnostic argue that child molesting priests should not be punished, or morally criticized, because child rape might be beneficial to kids in some other universe? We would view such ghastly equivocation as the sign of a bad conscience, and quite possibly a mental illness.

Agnosticism also faces the problem of the "null comparison." In computer languages, variables can be created called "variants," which can contain any type of data, from pictures to videos to numbers – the memory clipboard on your computer, used for copying and pasting just about anything, is an example of this. If you ask a computer to tell you whether the number two is equivalent to a "variant," the computer will tell you that this cannot be done, because you cannot be sure that the variant is in fact a number. If I ask you whether the number two is equal to "X," where "X" can be anything in the universe – or nothing at all – you will tell me that this fundamentally does not compute, and might wonder what kind of bizarre game I was up to.

"Is Susie an 'X'?" There is no way to know – if "X" equals "female" then yes. If X. equals "asteroid" then the answer is quite likely no. The question as it stands cannot be answered. This does not mean that Susie can be anything – this does not mean that Susie might be an asteroid as well as a female human being as well as a magical unicorn, a square circle and the pot of gold at the end of a leprechaun's rainbow.

You cannot compare anything to an unknown "X" – particularly something with known properties. The concept "deity" has specific properties, and cannot rationally be compared to some unknown alternate universe, about which we know nothing at all – the ultimate "X."

Thus the statement that gods might exist in an alternate universe is completely invalid, and entirely self-contradictory, since we are claiming to have some knowledge of existence and the specific properties of gods in some alternate universe about which we fully admit we know absolutely nothing, not even whether it exists. (Even the statement "an alternate universe may exist" is completely invalid, because existence is a property of *our* universe, and since we know nothing about an alternate universe, we cannot use the term "existence" to refer to anything about it.)

CLOSING THE OPEN DOOR

Imagine that you drive over to a friend's house to pick him up to go to a movie. You knock on the door, and he opens it.

"Let's go," you say.

He hesitates. "I can't go through that door," he says.

"Why not?"

He purses his lips and shakes his head. "Because it might be closed in some alternate universe..."

Would you accept this as a rational and healthy statement on the part of your friend?

Of course not. You would try to get him some professional help. You would be particularly concerned that he opened the door in the first place – thus indicating specific knowledge about its status – and only then got all foggy about whether it was opened or closed.

But this is *exactly* the position of agnostics! They open the door of reason and evidence in order to nullify reason and evidence. They use a rational argument to say that reason is invalid. They create evidence out of thin air which is the opposite of existence and essentially say that no conclusions can be made because existence might equal the opposite of existence.

Why is this so cowardly?

If the agnostic position is valid, and if agnostics genuinely believe that no positive conclusions can ever be achieved and maintained, then surely they have far more important things to achieve in this world, relative to their values, then haggling over possible sky ghosts in another universe.

Surely agnostics should be virulently opposed to the existing justice system, which puts a man in jail for life based on a videotape of him stabbing his wife to death. This is a far more immediate reality than whether Zeus might exist in Dimension X – yet I have *never* heard an agnostic say that we should never send anyone to jail, because even if this man undoubtedly murdered his wife in this dimension, he might not have murdered her in another dimension, and so we cannot say for sure that he is guilty.

I have never heard an agnostic refuse to go to a funeral, arguing that the deceased might still be alive in another universe.

I have never heard an agnostic refuse medical treatment, on the grounds that he might be perfectly healthy in Dimension X, or that what cures him here might kill him "over there."

I have never borrowed money from an agnostic, and have him accept my argument that I do not have to pay him back in this universe, since I might have already paid him back in another universe, and so he cannot say for sure that he has not been repaid.

I have never heard an agnostic tell a victim of abuse that she has no right to be upset, because in another universe, she might not have been abused, or abuse might be the opposite of abuse.

No, agnostics never ever advocate these or a hundred million other absurd, offensive and insane positions.

Why not?

Why would agnostics *only* apply this kaleidoscopic and fogging "alternate universe" theory to the most distant and incomprehensible of human conceptions – that of a deity – and not to the far more egregious, immediate and important concerns of human society?

The answer is obvious – because agnosticism would be revealed as absurd, offensive and ridiculous if it were applied even remotely consistently.

So the question still remains – why is the door left open only for gods, and nothing else?

The answer is equally obvious – because agnostics are cowards.

AGNOSTICISM AND FEAR

The magic fog machine of agnosticism only pumps its noxious gases into the religious realm – it's like a cloud that miraculously wraps itself only around priestly garments. The reason, of course, for the astounding specificity of the "alternate universe" argument is that religious people tend to get upset, offended, ostracizing and angry when told that God does not exist.

This has little to do with the non-existence of God, but rather triggers all the volatile emotions surrounding family, culture and community.

When a religious person is told that there is no God, what he hears is, "My parents lied to me."

A man who is told that there is no God no longer sees in the mirror a being with a glowing soul, but a cramped sub-species of superstitiously (and surreptitiously) indoctrinated livestock – lied to, bullied and controlled for the sake of material money in the here and now. He is revealed not as a free man, basking in the glory of the divine, but a mere slave to the lies of the priests, fed crippling falsehoods and fattened for the feast.

People do not really believe in gods, that is a basic reality of life – they *say* that they believe in gods because they are afraid of being attacked by others for expressing doubt, or thought. Religions are the ultimate case of the emperor's new clothes, an old fairy tale where thieving weavers pretend to make a suit for the King, claiming that anyone who is unfit to his position will be unable to see it. Naturally, everyone pretends to see the suit, and marvels at its fine colors, until a boy on the street innocently asks why the King is walking around naked.

If you walk up to a man and tell him that his parents lied to him about everything that is true and good and right in the world, and sold his hide to thieving priests because they were afraid to stand up for truth and virtue, naturally he will be very, very upset.

Clearly, this is why agnostics do their n-dimensional somersaults — to avoid the anger, offense and potential retaliation from the religious.

I have no particular issue with people who do not want to step into the boxing ring of philosophy — not everyone is suited for these kinds of conflicts, and certainly battling superstition is not a strict moral requirement. It can be extraordinarily uncomfortable to experience the disorientation, bitter anger and caustic ostracism shooting up from the deep well of discontent when you shine down the light of reason and evidence. It is not for everyone, it is not necessary, and one can live a virtuous and happy life without taking on this kind of combat.

The world is filled with countless wrongs that I do nothing to prevent or avenge — I do nothing to feed starving children in North Korea, and while I am unhappy that they are starving, I recognize that I have chosen not to help them. I think that I am doing my own part to advance the cause of truth, reason, virtue, evidence and philosophy in the world, and I am very proud of my achievements in these areas, but of course there are millions of wrongs I do nothing about, and I recognize the reality of that, and do not seek to make excuses about my choices.

Imagine that immediately after I said that I was doing nothing to help the starving children of North Korea, I immediately said, "But there is no reason to believe that they are actually starving, because in some alternate universe, they might not be hungry at all!"

Would this not be a rather bewildering statement for me to make? Why on earth would I need to create an alternate universe in which North Korean children were not starving?

Again, the answer is blatantly obvious – I need to create an alternate universe where North Korean children are not starving because I am *extremely* uncomfortable with not feeding them.

If I were at peace with my decision, I would not need to create an alternate universe wherein that decision would be unnecessary. It does not require a high level of psychological sophistication to understand that if I am unfaithful to my wife, and then I obsess over an alternate universe wherein I remain faithful to my wife, that my obsession is driven by guilt and shame and a tortured desire to have chosen differently in the past. It also is not the summit of psychological insight to understand that I have a need to create an alternate universe wherein I am faithful to my wife because I am fairly sure that I will be unfaithful to her again in the future, and am preparing the way for another transgression.

I do not have conclusive empirical evidence for this, but I have certainly experienced it during my many years of debating these issues, with friends and strangers alike, but my strong belief is that agnostics are secular-minded people who come from religious parents. Deep down, they fear – and I would imagine not unreasonably – that their parents will choose God over them, if faced with such a choice. This is a truly tragic situation, which I have not had to face directly myself, and my heart goes out to people caught in this supernatural trap. Agnostics and theists are caught in the endless and stagnant merry-go-round of "let's agree to disagree." Agnosticism is a way of fencing off a topic emotionally with a big cloudy fog bank upon which is inscribed the blurry letters, "Don't go there!"

The fact that agnostics only invoke alternate universes for gods indicates not that *I* think that agnostics are cowardly, but rather that they themselves are of this opinion.

I wish to reiterate that I do not think that it is cowardly to avoid confrontation with the religious – I can perfectly well understand why someone who has a reasonably good relationship with religious parents might wish to avoid confrontations about the nonexistence of gods. However, honesty is the first virtue, and the most important honesty is honesty with the self – if that is absent, everything that follows is false. The true reality for agnostics is that they do not wish to anger or upset religious people – I can understand that, but that needs to be admitted. Failing that admission, agnostics need to apply their "alternate universe" theories to everything, since it is a principle of epistemology, or fundamental knowledge.

To create a singular exception to a universal rule for that which makes you uncomfortable, rather than just admitting your discomfort, is dishonest and cowardly.

If an agnostic can honestly admit that he is afraid of confronting religious people, then he does not need to continue slithering through the foggy gymnastics of alternate universes and the certain knowledge of the uncertainty of knowledge.

Cowardice is the avoidance of honesty, not danger. A man who says he did not join an army because he was afraid of dying is being honest. A man who claims an imaginary illness – even to himself – is a liar, who is obviously uncomfortable with his own choices, and chooses to bewilder and confuse others rather than be honest at least with himself.

Agnosticism and Religion

Many agnostics will claim courage because they ridicule and attack organized religion. The fact that we cannot prove or disprove the existence of God, they say, has profound implications for human theology, rendering any specifics about gods or their properties utterly imaginary and foolish.

This, however, does not hold logically. The alternate universe theory, as discussed above, cannot be specific only to gods, but is a universal principle that applies to everything. When the agnostic says, "We cannot disprove the existence of gods," he is really saying, "We cannot disprove the validity of any statement."

This is the fundamental crux of the matter. Agnosticism cannot be a principle if it only applies to gods, and there is no logical reason why it should only apply to gods, and so *no human statement or belief or perspective or prejudice or bigotry can ever be proven or disproven*, according to agnosticism.

For an agnostic to say that organized religion is foolish runs entirely against the basic principles of agnosticism. If I believe that my God is an invisible spider that squats in my eardrum and whispers the truths of the universe only to me, how can this possibly be contradicted according to agnosticism? In an alternate universe, this could be exactly the case. The agnostic cannot say that this is definitively false, for the moment that definitive falsehoods can be identified, the alternate universe theory collapses.

This is what is so tragic about agnosticism: agnostics often think that they are undermining religious certainty, but the exact opposite is true. By saying that every conceivable human perspective could be valid in some alternate universe, agnostics raise rank subjectivism to the status of scientific objectivity, and madness to rational skepticism. An agnostic cannot say to a racist that he is wrong, because in some other universe, the despised race might in fact be inferior! This failure to identify and apply objective and consistent principles – the very essence of philosophy – not only drops any and all rational defenses against subjective bigotries, but rather spurs them on, and elevates them to the very heights of philosophical wisdom.

Finally, agnosticism is a snake that eats itself. If we say that no human statement of truth can ever be proven or disproven, what are we to make of that statement itself? Isn't this just another example of one of the oldest philosophical piles of sophist nonsense, the statement: "Nothing is true." Of course, if nothing is true, the statement that nothing is true is false, which is a self-detonating position.

In the same way that agnosticism creates this magical exception for the existence of gods, it must also by the very logic of its principles create a magic exception for its own arguments. The moment that we hear the word "except" in a philosophical statement, we know that we are in the presence of Grade A nonsense. "Nothing is true – except this statement!" Meh, that isn't even philosophy, that is just a Mobius strip fortune cookie.

In the same way, when agnostics affirm that no statement can be proven or disproven, are they creating a magical exception for that statement? If so, on what basis do they create this magical exception? If not, then do they recognize the ridiculousness of their position?

THE MISUSES OF HISTORY

When you are inventing a new idea, using the word that describes its exact opposite is a very bad idea. If I want to sell a dessert, I do not describe it as an appetizer, a mountain or a virus. If I want to sell a map, I do not describe it as a mystery novel, or switch North with South, East with West.

A man who wants to sell you something new, while describing it as something very old, is very likely a con man, looking to pass off a new table as an antique, or a cheap replica as the original.

Agnosticism is a relatively modern phenomenon; avoiding the question of God's existence is nothing new, of course, but agnosticism attempts to hook into a lot of science, particularly quantum physics, string theory and other multidimensional theoretical models.

This is little more than a transparent and obvious con.

Historically, the word "God" has never meant, "things that may exist in other dimensions of the multiverse, as described by modern physics." "God" has never referred to some unknowable X factor, Schrödinger's cat, the unified field theory, the cosmic craps player so derided by Einstein, or any of the other trappings of modern science.

No, let's not empty the word "God" of its true and original meaning, which was a cosmic and spiritual father who created the universe, breathed life into mankind, burns the wicked and saves the innocent, and so on. This meaty and monstrous superman, this thunderbolt-hurling patriarch of our dim and brutal histories, this frustrated and enraged slaughterer of rebels and sceptics – this fearful and omnipotent beast should not be reduced to some pale and conceptual ghost hiding out in the dim theoretical alleys between the atoms.

Using the word "God" to refer to some theoretical possibility of mind-bending modern physics is to take a word steeped in the superstitious blood of our earliest collective histories, and attempt to propel it like some time-bending slingshot forward into the future – an exercise in futility, since this old and very brittle word cracks and collapses in the face of such insane velocity.

When it was first discovered that the world was round and not flat, the word "flat" was not enlisted to describe the newly discovered roundness. When ancient mathematicians first invented the concept "zero," they did not attempt to reuse the number one to describe it – for the simple and obvious reason that if you attempt to use the same word to describe something very different, you will spend the rest of your life trying to slice and dice peoples comprehension of your meaning. "Wait, do you mean the word 'one' to mean the old number one, or the new symbol for zero?"

It is so obviously inefficient to use the same word for opposite things – or even different things – that we should be immediately suspicious when this problem arises. A man who proposes calling his wife his mother, and his mother his wife, is complicating not only his relationships, but also his psyche. A cab driver who tries to start using the word "uptown" to mean "downtown" will simply annoy his customers and lose his job.

The passionate, visceral, crazed and dangerous deities of the ancient world were called "gods." The word refers to Stone Age superstitions, not modern theoretical definitions of physics. "God" refers to not only a pre-scientific period, but an anti-scientific and anti-rationalist stage of our development, if development is even the right word. To the Egyptians of 6,000 years ago, the gods were living beings that you prayed to, feared, obeyed, and slaughtered virgins for. They joined you in war, contemplated healing you in sickness, cursed your enemies and strengthened your offspring. They did not hide in some possible alternate universe, waiting for almost 6,000 years for some scribbles on a mathematicians paper to reveal their potential hiding place.

We do not see agnostics attempting to rehabilitate the phrase "human sacri-fice" by referring to it as a synonym for benevolence, because the strangeness, irrationality and quite frankly psychological problems that would be revealed by such a goal would be far too obvious.

Agnostics do not strenuously advocate for the legalization of rape, arguing that it might be moral in some other universe – yet they strenuously oppose atheists who deny the existence of God. This is a most strange position to see – surely if evil might equal good in some other universe, then violently banning evil in this universe is utterly unjust! If certainty is impossible in this universe, then surely we should start by opposing violently enforced certainties – such as physical self-defense – rather than merely strongly word-ed opinions, such as the fact that gods do not exist.

Yet oddly enough agnostics slither right past violently enforced views such as the evils of rape, murder, theft, parking in a handicapped zone, the non-payment of property taxes, failing to come to a proper stop at a stop sign, speeding and everything else. All these legally enforced perspectives are ut-terly ignored, although they are inflicted with infinitely greater absolutism than a mere philosophical argument – and the agnostic reaches with open fingers for the throat of the mere atheist!

In other words, the violent *enforcement* of certain perspectives is perfectly acceptable to the agnostic, but mere *arguments* for other perspectives must be aggressively and endlessly opposed.

This is why I call agnosticism cowardice.

And if you are still an agnostic, after reading and failing to rebut these arguments, you have well earned the label.

Conclusion

The first virtue is always honesty, and the first honesty is always with the self.

I do not for a moment imagine that agnostics have reached their conclusions by dispassionately looking at the available arguments and evidence. Agnosticism – like determinism and other forms of self-detonating superstition, arises from a fear of social attack, and a staunch denial of self-knowledge.

If you do not have the stomach to encourage the potentially rational, expose the irrational and condemn the anti-rational, you have nothing to be ashamed of. I feel queasy at the sight of blood; I'd make a terrible surgeon – but I know and accept this fact, so I don't need to recast my queasiness as other-dimensional courage.

If you are afraid of sticking your neck out in this highly unprofitable realm, that's completely fine. If you're scared of how others may react to the truth, that's natural, normal and healthy. Just – accept that. We don't all have to be good at everything. Leave this heavy lifting to others. I don't drill my own cavities, and you can leave the perilous advancement of reason to the philosophers.

All that we ask is that you get out of the way.

Made in the USA
Las Vegas, NV
12 February 2023

67358674R00046